Anonymous

A History of God's Work Through His People for the Thornwell Orphanage

Anonymous

A History of God's Work Through His People for the Thornwell Orphanage

ISBN/EAN: 9783744753197

Printed in Europe, USA, Canada, Australia, Japan

Cover: Foto ©ninafisch / pixelio.de

More available books at **www.hansebooks.com**

THORNWELL ORPHANS' SEMINARY.

Almighty God Careth for Me.

A

HISTORY

OF

GOD'S WORK THROUGH HIS PEOPLE

FOR THE

THORNWELL ORPHANAGE,

BEING

THE TESTIMONY OF A GRATEFUL HEART.

CLINTON, S. C.:
THORNWELL ORPHANAGE PRESS.
1888.

INTRODUCING THE WRITER.

I am constrained to put the story of God's work for the Thornwell Orphanage into the shape of a personal narrative because it is so interwoven with my personal experience that there is no other way to do it. But I am to tell you not of what I have done, but of what the Lord has done for the cause that I love best of any in this world.

I propose to let you, my friendly reader, into the inner secrets of a history that is not full of startling adventure, or sudden surprises, or wonderful opportunities, but deals with what may be the experience of any one who will walk in the simple, plain path of that duty that comes to all alike.

George Muller, in the wonderful record of his great work in Bristol, England, declares that for his success he depended on prayer simply and only; that he made the Lord alone the recipient of the cry of his complaint; and that his great Orphan-Houses are not a testimony of the love of God's people for the orphan, but of God's willingness to answer prayer. How few there are that can attain to so magnificent faith! Yet that such is possible, his life-work wonderfully demonstrates.

Preface.

The lesson to be taught in the pages that follow, is slightly different. They will not only testify that God *is* a prayer-hearing God, but that also He has given His children a part in the work of his Church. Labor, to be acceptable to God, must have these qualities: it must be built on faith; baptized with prayer; wrought in humility, self-denial and patience. To all men, such labor is possible—even the humblest. The success that follows is a testimony that the blessed Saviour whom we serve is the living God.

CHAPTER I.

BY WAY OF GETTING THE STORY BEGUN.

IT is one of the most precious recollections of my life that I was ushered into this world amid the surroundings of a Christian home. I have often heard men boast from the pulpit of the vileness of their lives, from which the grace of God saved them. Even so noble a man as George Muller holds himself as a brand plucked from the burning. God does not call upon us to publish our shame abroad in this manner, even as He does not approve the Pharisee's prayer, "Lord I thank thee that I am not as other men are," or even of the young man's glad assertion, "All these have I kept from my youth up." I gratefully thank God that amid the innumerable things I have to thank Him for, one is that he shielded my early life from great sin, and brought me at a very early age to love the Lord Jesus Christ. I think his protecting care is as wonderfully manifested in covering the heads of his little children from every storm as in resuscitating blackened souls which the lightning of sin has scarred and scorched.

I remember when I was but a little lad how bravely I could lie alone in the night, banishing the goblins of the dark that an excited imagination and a naturally timid disposition would conjure up, by applying to my heart this thought,—"The Lord is the strength of my life, of whom shall I be afraid?" Nor has any thought been so strong as this through all the years that have followed. I have been in perils oft, but amid every danger from the flash of lightning, the wild beast of the forest, the storm-beat sea, or the mountain's slippery pathway, I have felt that "The Lord careth for me."

Reader, that sentence I wish to have in your lips as well as mine. It is the golden thread that binds the pages of this book together. It is the voice that is uttered from every stone that makes up the buildings of the Thornwell Orphanage.

Once there came to me this thought:—It God cares for me, ought I not to care for others? The first question that man ever put to God was this, "Am I my brother's keeper?" The last command ever given in holy writ answered it. "Let him that heareth say, Come!" It was that answer that lead me as a boy to work in the sunday-school, and while yet beardless, to endeavor to tell others of the goodness of God. It is needless to say that it was that which lead to this work for orphans. The Thornwell Orphanage has set to itself this delightful task,—to show to the Church its duty to God's helpless children, because he careth for us.

After graduating at Charleston College in 1861, I went, in the fall of the same year, to the Theological Seminary, Columbia, as a student for the Presbyterian ministry. The Professors at that time were, the modest, but withal profoundly learned Howe, the polished Leland, Woodrow the accurate and thoughtful, Adger, a very Nestor in things ecclesiastical, Cohen, the dispenser of Hebrew roots, and last, and though last, yet first, THORNWELL, idolized by us all as the Augustine, the Calvin, the Melancthon—all in one—of the Presbyterian Church.

On the 2nd day of August, 1862, I made this entry in my journal. I was not then a man as the law counts, but the impressions of early life become the profounder convictions of maturer years:

"The sad news reached us this day, of the death on yesterday, at Charlotte, N. C., of Dr. James H. Thornwell. As I write this sentence, my eyes are wet with tears and my heart depressed with sorrow. Confession like this is but the confession of many another throughout this South-land. The greatest man in the Southern Confederacy is dead. I saw him last just before the exercises of the Seminary closed for this session. Laying his hand on my head, he said solemnly,

"God bless, you, Bro. Jacobs, and make you useful." I will prize these words as the blessing of the greatest man that I have ever known. What a cause of regret to the world is this death! He was nature's nobleman. A more talented, and yet more humble man, I never heard of. A more genial companion, a sincerer Christian, could not exist. Dr. Thornwell is fit for Heaven, and now he is sitting down with Luther, Calvin and Knox; with Paul and Peter; nay, more, with the holy and ever beloved treasure of his heart, Jesus the Mediator of the New Covenant!"

The death of Dr. Thornwell was felt by all his students as a personal loss. When ten years afterward, I suggested this name as the one our Institution should honor, I felt as if it were almost a sacrilege to connect a name so dear to my heart with a fledgeling that the world thought would die in its infancy. The name of Thornwell has a ring in the ears of his old students that is unlike that of any other name. We think of him as the founder of modern Presbyterian modes of thinking.

CHAPTER II.

A VILLAGE CHURCH AT THE BOTTOM OF IT.

In 1864, the little village of Clinton sometimes asked itself if it were a village at all. About thirty families composed the hamlet. The worn out and broken down Laurens Railway dragged its slow length through it from west to east. The best men in the village were soldiers on the Potomac or about Charleston. Business was absolutely dead. The only life in the village was given it by a few godly women and a handful of Charleston refugees. It contained a small Methodist Church, a Presbyterian Church with 47 members, including soldiers, a school-house, and two Baptist churches in the suburbs, about four miles away.

On the 27th of May, the tercentenary of John Calvin's death (1564), Presbytery met to ordain me Pastor of this church, and of the churches of Shady Grove and Duncan's Creek, and on the next day, the 28th, I was formally placed in charge of the church.

I found a thoroughly disorganized community, a church that although it was nine years old, had not yet learned what it meant, to be a church of Christ. The town itself had a very unsavory name abroad, and was proclaimed by its enemies as "the worst hole in South Carolina." Liquor asserted its right to rule. Human life was not accounted high in value. Only a few days before the ordination, a murdered man was found on the church grounds. But there were some of God's own in Clinton, men and women with backbone, and these only needed a link to bind them together, a tool, as it were, with which to work, in order to pull down the wrong, and to erect in its stead the right.

I need not rehearse the eight years of pastoral labor that followed. First, we had a vigorous sabbath school planted. What wondrous changes that school has wrought! What faithful and rewarded toil has been bestowed through it upon our young people. The prayer-meeting followed with its hallowing influences. Then the church began to learn to give of its substance, a thing almost unheard of before. Even the great work of God among the heathen had often met the sneer of "Cui bono?" Who would have dreamed in those days that our church should yet strive to lead its sister churches of the Presbytery as a Missionary church and should rejoice to send one of its own sons to the forefront?

It would not be just to the memory of those days to forget how bravely the Church fought on the side of Temperance. Sometimes victory was snatched from us just as our hands touched it, but we knew the power of the Devil's curse of drink. The gallant Bell was our leader. True men stood with him, and at last after fifteen years of battle, the bar-rooms were closed, the town swept of its vileness as though a cyclone had struck it, and the keys turned in the lock of a Legislative enactment.

It may seem a little strange, but it is nevertheless true, that in those days our church needed to unite the people in matters of temporal progress. Of course she must provide a Cemetery for the dead. But she also did her part in giving Railroads to the living. It is not with boasting that this is written, but only as a candid fact of history, that Clinton was made a town, a town of happy homes, by the Presbyterian Church.

The village lies at an altitude of 800 feet above sea-level. Mountain breezes from far-away peaks sweep over it. Pure water and good health is the rule. I came first to Clinton because of these things needed by an enfeebled constitution. I found congenial spirits among my congregation. I accepted no inducements to go away because I loved them. I was willing to share their poverty and suffer lack of all things with them, believing that the time would come when I could demonstrate to the world that *a little village church could be made a tower of strength, a blessing to those within it, and a lighthouse to all about it.*

Why should our young ministers seek for fat places in the Kingdom of God; or why, with ambitious ideas filled, should they long for posts of honor and fame? It should content us to work just where the Master puts us, trusting Him that He who knows all our need, will give us fat things if they be good for us, and honor and fame therewith, if they be for His glory.

CHAPTER III.

THEY UNDERTOOK TO BUILD AN ORPHAN'S HOME.

I HAD always had a fondness for types. In earlier days I had been much about the offices of the Charleston *Courier* and the Columbia *Daily Carolinian*, serving as a Reporter. There I had gained some practical knowledge of the art, but it was not this inborn fondness for typography that induced me in 1866 to purchase a small press and a few fonts of type. I wished to have some means of laying printed thoughts before my people and the community. The True Witness, a little four-paged weekly, lived only a year. In 1867 it gave way to an agricultural paper, controlled by my brother. In 1871 the agricultural feature was dropped, the name was changed to OUR MONTHLY, and it eventually became what it is now, a vehicle for religious thought, and of information about the work we were trying to do as a church for the Master.

I found OUR MONTHLY an invaluable assistant. Through its columns the scheme was worked up for the establishment of the Clinton High School (afterwards College) Association, which has since done so much for the development of a Presbyterian College in this town.

In the October number, 1872, of OUR MONTHLY, the same in which the announcement was made of the organization of the Clinton High School Association, appeared an article under the head of "Christ's Little Ones." It was as follows:

"In 1832, a noble-hearted German, Immanuel Wichern, established a home for destitute orphan children on a plan of his own. He was opposed to the gathering together of a great crowd of children in one Institution, but was of the opinion that twenty-four was as many as ought to be crowded into one building. He was also of the opinion that the home should be largely self-supporting, at least to the extent of requiring the children to labor on the Rauhe House farm and in the shops and offices connected with it.

"Greatly would our heart delight us to have the same experiment tried in our own land * * * We proposed, two years ago, such an Institution under the fostering care of the Presbyterians in this State. Is there love enough for God's orphan children to enable us to give some of the little remnant of our former wealth for this noble purpose?"

This article was the result, trifling as it may seem, of six months of prayer, consultation and study. The very first entry in the records of the Thornwell Orphanage is to this effect:

[Extract from the Minutes of Session, Clinton Presbyterian Church.]

"Sept. 1, 1872. The Moderator stated that he had received a letter from Dr. J. W. Parker, of the Palmetto Orphan-House, inviting this church to co-operate in maintaining that home. During the discussion which ensued, the formation of an orphan's home under Presbyterian control, to be located in Clinton, was suggested. Much conversation was held on this point, and it was finally resolved that the Pastor should draft a plan to be presented at the next meeting, on which such a home might be established."

Owing to the sickness of the Pastor nothing was done till

"Oct. 20, 1872. The Pastor presented his report in regard to the Orphans' Home, which was very fully discussed and finally adopted."

Until the 8th of January, 1873, all the work of organization was carried out by the Session of the Clinton Church, but as it was deemed best that another organization should take its place, on the 8th of January, the Board of Visitors of the Thornwell Orphanage, was officially organized and held its first meeting.

My thoughts go up with sweet gratitude to God for the noble band of workers that on that day put their hand to the wheel. Foremost among us was the enthusiastic Bell, now we trust, among the glorified saints of God. There were the Holmeses, father and son, the older was the founder of the Clinton Church, the younger was the first Principal of our newly organized High School. There were also with us the energetic Phinney, the sagacious Boozer, the quiet, but faithful Bailey, the God-fearing Copeland, the three Youngs, not of one blood according to the flesh, but one in faith and hope and good works; McClintock and Foster, the aged and beloved and now glorified; Green, the thoughtful and zealous West. There, too, was Blakely the beloved. Alas, the grave has closed over him. His sun set at midday. There was Copeland the younger, wise in counsel, Bailey and McCrary, on whom the mantle of our sainted Treasurer fell. And afterwards there came to us Lee the Learned, and Owings the true and tried, and Watts who now leads the orphan lads to weedy battles. Faithful co-laborers! who could not accomplish projects for the Master with such as you to help? Month by month, through all these years you met and worked and prayed. Rain did not hinder you. You came when sick and tired and busy. You asked no glory; no reward; but only to stand by your Pastor, as one man, and like Hur and Aaron of old, to hold up his hands, when he was ready to faint.

I remember as though it were but yesterday, the assembly of this band of workers in my parlor. The plan was presented. The time came to vote upon it. It was a solemn moment. I told the brethren present that if they voted Aye, it meant that I and they must cast in our lot together for life; that we were the least among the thousands of Israel, that neither Pastor nor people were known to the Church, that our poor little congregation was struggling for very life, having just called its Pastor for all his time; and that we must look forward to years of unremitting toil. There was this to encourage,—the cause was one on which we could ask God's blessing, and assuredly if we asked, we should receive. The vote was taken. Each one present answered, Aye. And our dear Bro. Bell said, "Now, Brethren, forward!"

A few days afterwards OUR MONTHLY published the tidings. Our first article appeared in the *Southern Presbyterian*. The world knew that a little people in

Clinton had determined to lead the great Synods of South Carolina and Georgia, and God's people everywhere in a movement to extend the aid of the Church to the widow and the fatherless; the widow indirectly through her children. We wondered if the answer would be decisive.

To stand upon the mountain-top and look down over the vast prospect, one is overwhelmed for a moment with the glorious panorama. It seems an easy thing to have thus reached that high pinnacle; but to stand at the mountain's base and look up to its lofty crags, scanning the innumerable steps and besetting dangers that lie between, strikes the faint heart with dismay. Let not him that putteth off his armor boast as him that putteth it on; and, yet, poor as we were, we dared to boast! We dared to say of the long way to the mountain's crest,—"It is nothing!" Our soul did make her boast in God; and each one of us said, Where He leads, we will follow.

One of our earliest circulars closed with this sentence, "Dear friend, wherever you may be, pray for the success of our Orphanage. If you cannot give silver and gold, give us at least your prayers. If you pray aright, God will turn these prayers of yours into silver and gold, for He has the treasury, and He is the God of the fatherless."

And, yet, when this was resolved on, and when these trustful words were written, there was not one dollar in the treasury, nor promise of one. It is easy to believe after the event. We were called to believe, and to risk our all upon it, where, as yet, no ray betokened the coming sun.

CHAPTER IV.

THE STORY OF THE LITTLE RED LEDGER.

There lies before me as I write, a little red ledger of 200 pages.

The hand that made the entries in it is now silent in the dust. It is the account book of Wm. B. Bell, Treasurer. On that first day of October, 1872, when we held our informal meeting, needing something for postage and printing, we chipped in our dollars to the little collection basket. On this first page I find this first record, Wm. B. Bell, $1.00.

I turn the page, and now the accounts of the Thornwell Orphanage begin. I read, Willie Anderson, 50 cts. I remember it all. We were sitting at a widow's fireside. The Orphanage (at most an unknown word) was the topic. Little Willie put one arm on my shoulder and the other hand fast gripped about something in my lap. "Well, Willie, lad! what have you there, and what is it all about?" He blushed and opened his hand, and there lay in the orphan's palm that silver half-dollar. It was the first gift that came. It was the first drop of the shower.

I can cover with my hand every entry on the first page of this ledger, and yet it is the record of *two month's gifts!* Seventy-eight dollars and sixty cents in all. There are just twenty-five entries. The first gift by mail is James McElroy, of Charleston. Here is Dr. B. Adger, $5.00. It was the sole return for the first public speech I ever made for the orphans. Scene: Columbia Church; the Synod in session. Dear Bro. Riley had just helped us much with this resolution,

Resolved: That the Synod of South Carolina heartily approves of the proposition to establish the Thornwell Orphanage under the care of the Presbyterians of this State, and commends it to the Christian liberality of our people.

The resolution was voted in by a few feeble ayes,—no nays. Then our dear old professor rose and backed his vote with his dollars.

On that same little page I find that there were gifts from other states than our own; a nameless friend from New York, another from Maryland; three from Illinois, one from the District of Columbia. Strange enough, all were from states that might have been called the hostile North. The other gifts of those two months were mainly from our little village.

Friendship Church, in Laurens County, was the first church to take up a formal collection.

What heart-stirring thoughts swarm up from the pages of this little red Ledger! How we thumbed and studied those pages to see whether we with our little company of donors could turn an army of doubters into friends! What searchings of heart! What prayers! The names we read, too! Of this first page of helpers, heaven has reaped a harvest. Twelve out of the twenty-five are among the saints of God.

But the year 1873 opened with much encouragement. Gifts from Clinton first came in. Mississippi responded. Laurensville Presbyterians bade us God speed with a goodly list of Donors. Friendship, which church I was then supplying for a Sunday in each month, filled up a page. The month footed up $160. The showers were falling.

The whole of this first year of effort was occupied in raising funds for the purchase of a piece of ground on which to build. Many lots were examined. The one at last chosen is a beautiful spot along Broadway, Clinton. It is an irregularly shaped block of land, containing 125 acres, part woodland, part open, near the railway station, not far from the church. The Lord himself seemed to have directed us to it. Time was offered us in which to pay for it, and fifteen hundred dollars was set as the price By the first of August, twelve hundred dollars, all our collection, had been deposited in the savings bank at Laurens C. H. On the 8th of August, the gentleman from whom the titles were to be had, rode into Clinton and offered these titles to the Board on payment of the full amount. It was determined to close the trade at once; the $375 necessary to that end was borrowed, and that with a check on the savings bank was tendered in payment. To our surprise this latter was refused. And along with it the demand that the payment must be made that day or the trade would be off. Vexed at what seemed trifling, there was nothing for it but an immediate ride to Laurensville, nine miles away. Even there, difficulties awaited the collection of money from the bank. Wearied with the day's work, the settlement was at last made and the titles passed. What gratitude filled our hearts when we found, a few days afterward, that the Bank had closed its doors and gone into bankruptcy. Then we knew that our Orphanage had been saved. Was it by an accident? Nay, verily,—by the direct intervention of the good hand of our God. The gentleman from whom we purchased, had "builded better than he knew!" The Lord had sent him.

The year closed with the report from the Treasurer that he had received in the twelve-month, $1360.

A part of this had been received as the result of addresses delivered at Friendship, Laurensville, Greenwood, Newberry, Shady Grove, Charleston, Rocky Springs, and elsewhere, but the greater portion was the result of the warm-hearted work of many who now enrolled themselves as co-workers with us. I read over the list of our earlier helpers amid thanksgiving and tears! I see loving hands that helped in the toiling, now crossed forever upon the breast. But there are some who still abide. One young lady, Miss Lizzie Brearly, of Sumter, appears in the records of each year's work. Little by little, she has collected more than six hundred dollars.

CHAPTER V.

STONE AFTER STONE FROM THE QUARRY.

ANOTHER year had opened.

As yet we had lived by faith only. The time had now come to arise and build.

Early in 1874, a pair of oxen was purchased; Mr. G. C. Young's granite-quarry, freely tendered, was a busy scene of blasting. In the first week of the new year the first load of rock was delivered. Having decided to build of granite, we were now hard put to it to find workmen. Workmen in stone were not to be had. It was our heart's desire to build solidly, and yet the prospect was against us.

It was then that one of those singular coincidences occurred that compel us to believe that the Lord was caring for us On the 28th of January there arrived a batch of forty-eight emigrants, the first that had come and the last to come. Among these, two excellent stone masons were found. These two were to build the Orphanage, and then to disappear as they came, one to parts unknown and the other in the silent grave.

We had no architect. It was proposed to build simply and cheaply and as we received the money. We began without a dollar in the treasury. We only knew that God was helping us. We do not blame others because they could not see anything but foolhardiness in our plans. They looked at the men. They could not see that the men were looking at God. A friend of mine stopped me on the street one day and begged me to give up this project. Said he, "It will ruin you!" I told him "It were well to be ruined working for God." He shrugged his shoulders and turned his back. Another bantered me with the loan of ten dollars, at double interest, I *not* to return it if the Orphanage should ever be opened. I took the money. He has given up hope of seeing it.

At length the 28th of May had dawned upon us. It was the 10th anniversary of my ordination. How time was passing! The day was a lovely one. At the Methodist Church a great crowd of people were assembled. They wore the regalia of the Good Templars and Grangers and were from all parts of the country. Forming in procession, they were joined by bands of children bearing sunday-school banners. They marched down Main Street. When opposite the Masonic Lodge, that fraternity fell into line. The roads were filled with carriages; the sidewalks with people. This was the day we had been planning for. The friends of the Orphanage were gathered to testify their willingness to work. The Cornerstone was laid at 12 M., Hon. B. W. Ball presiding. A great feast was spread by the Ladies' Society of Earnest Workers, and best of all, nearly six hundred dollars was that day placed in the treasury. The immediate results of the day was to give us courage to go forward. The Lord was giving us favor in the sight of His people, and the people were giving us their money. Col. Ball, on leaving Clinton that evening handed me a bill for the treasury. Speaking of it afterwards, he said,—"I did it to encourage you all, not that I thought the Orphanage would ever be built." Oh God, bless these dear friends, and remember it for their good, even though their faith was in men and not in Thee!

When the first of October came, completing the second year of our orphan work, our Treasurer reported $1,846 as the receipts. Here was progress. Our land with accrued interest and taxes had all been paid for, and the Home of Peace had been completed to the level of the second story. We were working upward.

It would not be true to say that in all this time we had no anxieties. But there was never a doubt but that God would bring us to the accomplishment of our desires. Our fear was that we should not please God. We knew that God would help us, if we acted honorably toward Him.

We had set the first day of January, 1875, as the day of our opening. But Messrs. Young and Bell, who now contracted to build the house, were delayed in their work. Again we hoped that the 28th of May would see the doors open. Again hope deferred made the heart sick. In the meanwhile, orphans were applying for admission, and friends were asking "When?" and "How Long?"

The delay was better for us than we knew. Our own minds were not all of a unit. I felt that I wanted to swing clear away from the traditional Orphan Institution, and to found a Home-School that would have nothing of the Employment-bureau about it. I never could see why orphans should be treated like criminals, or made to feel that they were objects of charity. Throw up your hands in holy horror at that iconoclastic error! But I stand to it You shall not treat my children as though they deserved nothing but pity. They shall hold up their heads. They shall feel that they are men. Bind them out! Nay, verily, not if I live to prevent it. I am writing about my own flesh and blood, and am not saying this of my orphans. And, yet, why not of my orphans? *They* are God's children, and shall not God's children be treated as well as *mine?*

At length we all came to an understanding. We were to have a new idea for the world's people to cry down. The Church, the dear old Presbyterian Church, (God bless her) was to adopt these orphans; they were to be her own; she was to put spirit into them; to give them a true home; to educate them well, to do the best for them in that line that could be done; and having so fitted them for life's work, training head, heart and hand, to bid them God-speed as they took up their weapons and entered into the battle of life. We were to have our children to work;—yes,—work is noble; Jesus worked. It would make them feel honest, independent, self-reliant, to work. But there was to be no reformatory discipline; no institution-life; no law or ordinance that my own children could not endure.

There was another hindrance. We had no Matron. We had tried one and another. We had failed everywhere. One letter was sent to us that had it been received, would have prevented what afterwards happened. But it was missent to another office, though most plainly directed. In the meanwhile, the first of October was nigh at hand. It was the day fixed for opening.

It was most unexpectedly to me that she who now for nearly eleven years had been to me "starlight, moonlight, sunlight" *freely offered herself*. I could not understand it all at first. It seemed hard to give up a sweet home, a cosy fireside, my literary leisure, and to mix up my little ones with the children of strangers. Ah! were they not God's children? "Was there a lamb in all his flock, I would disdain to feed?" And so it all came about in God's way, which was wiser than our way, that we were to come close in to the heart of the work.

As September drew to its close, the contractors were prepared to give us the use of the building. We were $2,000 behind in the payments for it; but no papers were passed; there was nothing to bind us or any one. Already several orphans were at my house ready for the transfer. The third year ended, and the Treasurer reported. One large gift of five hundred dollars from "A friend in earnest" had been received. It cheered our hearts. This had been set aside for the endowment of the Orphanage. Besides, we had received $2,837.25, For all this I had made personal appeal to no one. I had laid our wants before God's people through the printed page, and left the rest with them.

Three long years of patient labor! Brethren beloved, my fellow workers together with God, how often I have thought over those years of the trial of our patience! They seemed hard then. But the Master was refining us, and fitting us to understand that His care of us does not preclude us altogether from the ills of life. It is even said that whom the Lord loveth, he chasteneth.

CHAPTER VI.

AT LENGTH THE GLAD DAY CAME.

SHALL I ever forget that first day of October, 1875? That day, the dream of five years and the toil of three, were to meet in a waking reality.

There was another great gathering. From all about us, and from every house in Clinton, came donations for the orphans. Little children brought chickens and eggs. One brought a coffee grinder, another a sieve, and so on. The older people brought barrels of flour, a great tub of lard, rolls of yellow butter, a hogshead of syrup, clothing, bed-quilts. I see now the beaming face of dear "Aunt Sake" (she was Aunt Sake to all of us,—a very mother in Israel) as she busied herself in sorting the great pile of things and

HOME OF PEACE

arranging them for the eye of a curious public. Blessed woman! you have passed beyond the stars, and the heavens hold you, but earth still cherishes your precious memory. You were the Deborah and Dorcas of our Israel, and tears rained down, when the clods covered you.

But from afar came gifts also. How cosy our bright little school-room looked, with its new furniture from the pious women of the old Second Church of Charleston. There was another Charleston church (Glebe St.) that had fitted up a room for the first group of orphan girls. Laurens and Cross Hill had done their part. Clinton had filled the kitchen and larder. Aveleigh spread the dining-room table. It was our joy, too, to welcome Rev. James H. Thornwell, on whom the mantle of his father's heart rested. My own dear father, an old man then, his head now whitened with 80 winters, was there to give his paternal blessing.

The day and the labors of preparation prostrated me; and I could take no part in the public ceremonies. But when night fell, there was a little gathering about my sick bed. Nearest sat the precious wife, whose love and wise thoughtfulness had made me what I was that was worthy; my own little band of four gave way for the time, that a half timid circle of little ones might press about her. There was little Ella, with her round bright face; Fannie and Mattie, our "elder sisters," sat next. Walter stood behind. Alfred was already tall, and his face showed the honor that was in him. There too was Johnnie, as full of fun as the days were long; Flora, bright, impulsive, earnest; and Annie, the sweet little pet of the household,—these made up the happy group that formed that first night's opening audience. Lowry, the hopeful, earnest young Christian, who presided over our High School (he is a Pastor now) and Miss Emma, whom the children loved from that very night as teacher seldom is loved:—these all knelt together, as I, prostrate in bed, bound them together with cords of faith.

They have all gone out from the home nest, but there is not one of that little company that has not been true to God and duty. Married people are they now. One of that group is waiting for us in heaven.

We began this work all so new, with heavy pressure on us of a debt of $2,000, which all our money receipts were pledged to satisfy; the building itself was unfinished and in the woods. But the Lord had touched our hearts and made us willing to bear and to work. Every shoulder was put to the wheel. The little ones that were with us caught at once the spirit of the enterprise. They were to be color-bearers.

One day, as I was sitting in my library, the little girls of the household came in, in a body.

"Heigh!" said I. "What is the meaning of this committee of the whole?"

Mattie was spokesman.—"Mr. Jacobs, what does it cost to feed one of us a year?"

"Well, my little one, I hardly know how to guage your appetites, but I guess, all round, about sixty dollars."

"And what do you have to pay the old Mauma that cooks for us?"

"There," said I, "you get me. Let me see, sixty dollars in money, sixty dollars in what she eats, and I really do not know how much in 'pickings and scrapings.'"

She clapped her little hands in glee. "Mr. Jacobs, this is what we have to offer! Send off the cook, and take two more orphans, and let us do the cooking!"

Ah, how proudly that fair young face shone as she tried to stretch up her lithe young form an inch or two higher. Blessings on the child!

That was the way it all came about that our girls took hold of their duties. The boys were not to be behind, and when January came, a "colored brother" had to seek another position. The children were divided into companies of twos and threes, each with a child-monitor in charge. What an easy time President and Matron were having! The children were running the machinery of the Institution.

It was just before Christmas that the Lord sent Bro. Tom Scott to us. Who is Tom Scott? Not to know him argues yourself unknown. Well, Tom Scott was everything. He had even tried to teach school. He was a painter. He was a trader. He had once been born in London. He was wide awake all over. He loved the Orphanage with all his heart. He was very fond of reading history. He knew just how to collect money. He didn't care a straw for worldly pelf. He did'nt expect to get married.

You say, That account is very much mixed up. So was Tom Scott. But the Lord had use for him.

I remember when he came to me once and said,—"You preached last night that the Lord would take any sort of a man?" "Yes." "That he would give his salvation to any that wanted it?" "You are right." "That he only asked in return an entire surrender?" "I did." "Then," he answered, "give us your hand on that—I take him at his word!" A few days after he united with the Church, he came back. "You said in your sermon last night that the Lord had use for everybody." "Yes." "Then here I am. Give me His marching orders."

And so our dear faithful, willing, energetic brother threw in his lot with us as general fac-totum, super-cargo, steward and right hand man.

That year passed quickly and busily by. New children came. Many friends bade us God-speed. Little improvements were added.

God's people had come to our help. $1,687.22 had been given to the support fund. A "friend in earnest," the same whose generous gift had given life to our enterprise, now added a Thousand Dollars to our endowment fund, while nearly, if not fully, fifteen hundred dollars worth of provisions and furniture and clothing had been sent in. It so happened that it was during that year that we needed much of this latter class of gifts, for all our cash receipts were to go to meet our indebtedness to our contractors. Was it not wonderful that God who alone knew this, should have provided for the wants of our household in a way that he has never done since, and thus enabled us to sweep away the burden of debt. Shout it to the heavens, oh men, and sing it, ye seraphs, God careth for us!

CHAPTER VII.

THE CHILDREN'S FOUNDATION.

When it was first proposed to found an Endowment Fund for the Orphanage, some objected. Was it not better to walk wholly by faith and not at all by sight? Would it not be better for both the Orphanage and the Lord's people that the one should depend for daily bread upon the other? It would give occasion for the continual exercise of Christian charity. George Muller decided against endowment. And, indeed, there is much to be said on that side.

But there is likewise much to be said on the other. God's care is as much needed to preserve buildings and endowments as it is to give daily bread. God's mercy is as much shown by giving one as the other.

This thought came to me,—Why not have both? There are certain promises that must be made in order to have efficient work,—such as the salary and support of matrons and teachers, There is also the need of frequent repairs and incidentals that do not appeal to the sympathies of God's people. We thought to raise a fund that we have fixed at Fifty

Thousand dollars, (the tenth of which has been received) to meet these lesser bills, and to provide that, come what might, the support of a number of orphans would be assured. This would give a nucleus only, leaving great margin of percentage for the exhibition of the charities of God's people.

Now, I want to say here, once for all, and with an emphasis as violent as a peal of thunder, that our experience has shown a thousand times over, that God answers prayer. On the truth of that proposition one may dare hang his faith in God's word, and in consequence, the salvation of his soul. All men's experiences may not be alike. But this has happened to me till repetition would make it a weary tale;—I have needed, say, $200 for some special object, perhaps to meet a call for provisions. I have asked just that money of my God, telling Him the day and hour when I must have it. The answer came in such a way that sent the electric flash of conviction to my soul that God was caring for us. It was no distrust of Him, therefore, but what we believed to be the guidance of His providence that led to the founding of our endowment.

And here a difficulty met us.

There was coming upon us the care of an annually increasing family that needed large gifts for their support. An appeal for an endowment would cut off this support. Personal appeals I would not make. Indeed I could not, for my pastoral work, my frequent preaching, and now my personal care of the Orphanage household, forbade any such endeavor.

Then it was remembered that the first three gifts to the Orphanage were from children. "Why cannot our children the youth of our Sabbath-schools, give us an endowmeut?" That settled it.

So the inuumerable mites began to flow in. I look through the veil upon a picture. I see multitudes of pure, sweet hands of childhood ministering! They are piling up little pyramids of pennies, nickles and dimes. They are building up the "Children's Endowment Gift." Angels are hanging over it. It is as sweet incense before the altar of God.

Thus we began the new year with this new plan to win the sweet hearts of God's blessed children to do work for children. It was my own sabbath-school that laid in the first gift in the foundation of this enterprise. Even the orphans helped to swell the gift.

We also found that this new movement did not interfere with the support of our household. Now, first, also, the plan inaugurated by the dear old 2nd Church, of Charleston, of selecting one child to be supported by a society, church, sunday-school or individual. This is after the manner of an endowment that brings us very near to the people of God. Their love is our endowment. The interest comes with a steady flow. In that first year, there were four churches and individuals to take up this work for God, and all four abide with us to this day.

The year was an uneventful one of steady work. God's little children paid into their gift fund, $333.10 The receipts for the support amounted to $1,458. A friend gave $100 to finish off the attic story of the building. A Charleston gentleman presented a $200 bond to our Endowment. A change had also occurred in our household. Miss Thornwell had taken the place of our first teacher, Miss Witherspoon. She was rapidly winning her way to our hearts.

I love full well to tell of the goodness of God to these children. But I love better still to tell these fatherless ones, as I meet them each day, of what the Lord is doing for them. To care for an orphan's body is an easy matter. Indeed, a little roughness will drive him to do that for himself. To cut and polish the bright gem of his mind till it shines with thousand-faced lustre, that is labor. But there is a secret still beyond this. It is to find the child's soul and to hold it up to the eternal Sun, till a light comes down into it that innumerable storm-clouds can only make to burn the brighter.

God seems to say to me every day, "Teach my children my law!" It was for this that the Thornwell Orphanage was founded, and it must *save* the children. There has never passed a year since the opening that some of the orphans have not pressed into the Kingdom, yet there has never been a "revival" among them. It has been so easy for them to feel that they are God's own precious children. They attend the church and sunday-school as equals with others. They mingle freely in social intercourse with Clinton people. No badge was set upon them. They were not marked and labelled as "Orphans." They were not orphans,—God is their father. *Therefore*, they must love Him and serve Him. Of the twenty-one children that began our third year with us, every single one became a member of the church.

The year was one of quiet, faithful, persistent labor. The school was putting in telling work. The children daily rolled up their sleeves and went at it like little men and women in Kitchen, Laundry, Garden and Printing Office. If the thoughtless grumbled, the older silenced them. "God is caring for us," they said, "we must do our part." Manual labor schools are usually a failure. The motive is absent. But here the motive is,—"Because God and His Church are helping us, we will help ourselves. To the work! To the work!"

The eyes of my readers would be weary if I were to spread before them all the incidents of each passing year. The improvements of those early days were effected through great toil. I remember taking a friend to the front of the building., He noticed five bolt holes through the stone wall.—"What are they for?" "They are left to bolt the frame work of the wooden piazza to the stone work, when we build one." "When you build one?—It will never be built!" But it was built, and a neat little kitchen tacked on at the rear of the house. They cost only $300. We thought we were doing great things then. And were we not?—The Lord had given us twenty-one precious children to train for the Kingdom, and $1,949.31, wherewith to make provision for them.

CHAPTER VIII.

A THICK CLOUD.

MY neighbor who has lost a little finger, tells me that he misses it every day,—he feels as though a great part of him were gone.

I never dreamed when 1879 dawned upon our happy household, that the desire of my soul and the staff and stay of those many orphans should with speaking eyes, wave us a fond farewell, as she placed her frail hand in God's. Blessed Master, the misery of that hour could never have been borne, but for the other arm wherewith Thou didst bear up the sufferer. It was a time of solid darkness that encompassed him, with only the little light within the soul, where Thou didst dwell, oh my God.

Pardon me, my reader. I have no right to say these things here, but that I saw the orphans, orphaned again, their tears washing the face of her who had loved them so, who had given up all for them, and whose fair hand would nevermore caress them. God pity the man who loses a faithful wife. God pity the children that lose a faithful mother.

FAITH COTTAGE

We buried her. And then all the beauty in the children's character shone out. Our zealous teacher, Miss Thornwell, with courage worthy of her glorified father, took all the tasks of the house upon herself. The children went like clock-work with a soul in it, to their duties. And when Mrs. Lee came to take the reins in her hand, it seemed as natural a transition as for to-day's sun to follow yesterday's.

There was a little lad that had come to our Orphanage, who from the very first had won his way to our hearts. Little Frank loved everything. He would put his arms about the neck of "Calfie" and pour his words into its senseless ears. If the pigs saw him they ran squealing after him. They knew who was their friend. He would fill his hands with fodder and hunt up "old Charlie" that he might see him happy with his crunching of the crisp blades. Every dumb thing, and things that were not dumb, loved him. Frank's story was a long one and a sad one. I need not tell it. We called him "our little Spaniard" for Frank's mother was a Castilian, and his birth-place Mexico, and thither he fondly dreamed he would one day carry the story of Jesus. But the Master had chosen Frank to keep company with his dear second mother in heaven. (Oh, how she loved him!) It was on the 8th of September that the wild alarm wrung a storm of tears from the eyes of our orphan household,

—"Frank is dying! Surely he is dying, for we cannot wake him!" And then a few moments after, "Frank is dead?" He had passed away and none knew what ailsd him.

In those days God was teaching us to say, "Shall we receive good at the hand of God, and shall we not likewise receive evil?" I copy this sentence from Frank's Bible. Years ago his little hands turned its pages. To-day, if we could be with him, he could explain to us that soul-piercing mystery.

How quickly these children, gathered from many States and different surroundings, learn to love each other. They are not strangers. Their attachments become like bars of iron for firmness. Alone in the great world, the heart cries out for partnership. They find it in this sweet home-circle and are glad. Let none wonder, then, that this dear child should have been mourned with love that was true and deep.

Who would have thought that a little life like that of Frank's should have had a noble purpose to serve in the economy of God's Kingdom. Yet, it was to be even so.

A dream had come into our hearts that possibly some day God would open up a way to add a second cottage to our establishment, in which a family could be set off for themselves. We had put it aside as not to be thought of. When, however, Mrs. Burt, of Philadelphia, sent us a check for $155 43 to be used as a memorial of little Frank Cripps, we saw that God's time had come. We did not know just whence a sum of which that would be one-tenth, should come; nor did we wish to make special appeals for it, for fear (how little we knew God's Church!) that we would be thought too avaricious for the fatherless. And so we lay the matter before God and asked His guidance. By faith the walls of Jericho fell down, and by faith can these walls be built up. *Faith Cottage* shall it be called. "Ask and ye shall receive," our motto.

So the Board said to me, "Go forward!" and I obeyed. The boys themselves were filled with enthusiasm for the scheme. The wagon was put to its best work to haul in rock for the building. Clinton sent her teams to aid us.

The year 1880 dawned upon us and found us busy. The whole of the previous year had only placed $1763 in our treasury. The annual income had been decreasing for two years. Times were very hard.

Often we needed to go to go to God for strength. We had met with newspaper persecution. Friends had grown cold. Death had done its sad work in our household. But what is faith worth if it cannot see in the dark. Lord, Thou didst mean to teach us that no stone should go into these buildings that Thou didst not place there. If this was to be God's work why should he not do it in His own way? His way might puzzle the workmen. Let them wait. They would thus best learn that it was Another working, and not themselves. Were there no hindrances, there could be no faith.

Inch by inch the new building progressed. On the 28th of July our church filled out the 25th year of its organic life. The afternoon of that day was selected as a suitable occasion to put the corner-stone in place. It was exceedingly unlike the former ceremony Now, only the Church took part. She had given it birth. She now blessed it with her prayers. But around the President was gathered a happy group of four and twenty orphans, whose voices were lifted up to the blue skies in sweet thanksgiving.

Bro. Scott builded with his own hands and infused heartiness into the workmen. The methods of concrete building had to be studied and then put into practice. It was well and faithfully done. The annual "New Year's Day," Oct. 1st, brought the Board together to hear the sum of their 8th year's work.

Summing Up.

See what God and faith had wrought. For Faith Cottage, $1,072.34 had been received. To the endowment $447.59 had been added. While for the support fund the gifts had run up to $2,185.78. Evidently it would not be a mistake to enlarge the number of our wards.

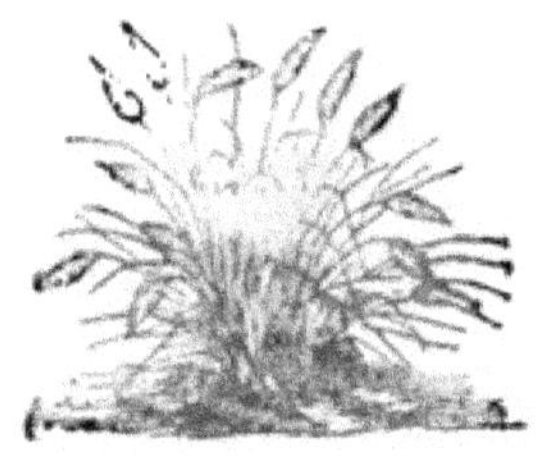

CHAPTER IX.

LENGTHENING OUR CORDS.

A MARBLE slab with this simple inscription

FAITH COTTAGE

1880

Ask and ye shall receive

Is seen by any one who ascends the steps into the portico of that building. Lest men should be silent, the stone utters its testimony to the goodness of God.

On the 21st of March, 1881, our hive swarmed, and the boys, with genial, kind-hearted Gus Holmes as their elder brother, moved in, bag and baggage. The little printers shouldered their type cases, their galleys and their shooting sticks. The great press was mounted on a wagon and escorted over in state. The President's office was lodged in the "parlor" and the press in the "kitchen."

On that day, when all the bills were in and the workmen dismissed, we found that all accounts footed up $1500.38, and our receipts showed just 1500.38 to meet them.

We had gathered of God's manna in our vessels of Faith, anh lo! there was no lack, neither was there any over.

Would you like now to walk in among the children and see them for a moment, as we leave these shifting scenes behind us. Some that we met five years ago, are gone. Little Annie is now a sweet, fair-faced young lady; this is Mollie,—Ah, Mollie, we little thought you and Gus would play us such a trick. Married, eh? I do not think one could help loving Minnie,—"little" Minnie we called her, (what is that? *you* would'nt call her so?) Here too is our poetess; and this one is to be our old maid; and this one makes the little boys stand around (she is in Arkansas now). You want to see the boys? They are gone to Enoree to-day. Up long before day. Even staid Sam is with them; Darby, and Will, and Tom, and Ben, and Allie, and Ellerbe, and the rest of them. Off for a royal fish and a plunge in the rushing waters. We can trust them, never fear, if *they are orphans!* Ah, boys, you are all men now.

"Swifter than a weaver's shuttle" (so says the blessed Word), are our lives. We felt it to be so, and when, just after the doors of Faith Cottage were opened and the lads trooped in, there came a new cry to us,—"Our school-room is too strait for us. We be too many!"

We had cleared away the rubbish and moved aback of the new building, the embracing fence. That night the Board met. I thought to burst a bomb-shell among them. "Brethren," I said, "our school-room is too small. Our classes tread upon each other. We need a school-house; one worthy of the name of Thornwell, with hall and library, museum and class-rooms." The bomb-shell didn't burst. "We knew it," they said, "it is high time!" They had faith. If they could trust me, could not I trust God? I laid the matter down at Jesus' feet. I told Him what His orphans needed. And He too knew it before I did. "Then, Master, lead and let me follow!"

While I was rousing up to this new toil,—that year, the 9th year of our endeavor, the 5th of our orphan-work, ended. God had given me $2.244.19 for the orphans, $500 for Faith Cottage and $1.644.96 for the endowment. And there had also been, while I waited, $106 sent in for the new building.

I look over those figures for the endowment, and I read between them a golden thread of providence. At one end Mrs. Nettie F. McCormick is disentangling the skein, Judge Cothran aiding, and presently the knot falls apart, and a thousand golden dollars pour down into the orphans' treasury. The Lord is able to help by few as well as by many. One can chase a thousand, and two put ten thousand to flight.

For a second time the Master has sent a liberal donor to build up our endowment. And this too, was a woman. Forget not this, it was a woman that brought into the world the Son of God!

How deep is a human heart! None can see the storms of the soul. Neither can any see its sunshine. It is easy now "to build the Orphans' Seminary" on paper. But the work of building in stone and mortar was not so easy. From October to March we were busy collecting money and material. The boys were giants among the rocks. Ben was famous among the boys, and boasted with honest pride of the great loads he hauled. Mr. Scott took charge of the workmen. We were to build a great house. It was to be the largest of the buildings, with a handsome hall for gathering, and a bell tower from which we were to see the mountains. We began the work with but little money. Why should that trouble us? We would not need to pay the workmen till Saturday. If our Master thought best, we could stop the work whenever it pleased Him. It was His work, not ours. If it went forward, there were to be 94 weeks (we didn't know it then), at the end of every one of which His Bank must honor our drafts.

Now this is the proposition. We were to erect and furnish a house that would cost us more than Five

Thousand Dollars. We must receive, then, on every Saturday for 94 weeks, sixty dollars, over and above the cost of caring for a household of more than forty persons. How often it happened, that on Monday morning, when the workmen assembled, there was not a dollar in the treasury. And yet, never once was a hand turned away unpaid on Saturday night, or his pay kept back for a single hour. Even the most astonishing surprises lose their force as they become the usual current of affairs. But the demonstration loses none of its force to those who were actors here. We have just taken it now to be the most natural thing in the world to believe this true thing: There is a God on earth and he cares for us.

We laid the corner-stone of the Orphans' Seminary in the presence of a great crowd on the afternoon of our eighteenth sunday-school anniversary, May 11th, 1882. We love thus to run our memories together. Mrs. Thornwell, the venerable widow of the honored and illustrious, was with us. Bell, now of the Church triumphant, laid the stone in place. The orphans sang out their joy, and the multitudes added,

Praise God from whom all blessings flow,
Praise Him all creatures here below,
Praise Him above, ye heavenly host,
Praise Father, Son and Holy Ghost.

On the 17th of September, the last stone was put into the walls, the masons discharged, and the carpenters called in. Six months of work condensed into six lines. From that completed wall went up this cry, "Master, I need three thousand dollars more. To Thee this is nothing. Lord, open Thy people's hearts that they may pour out the treasure." That prayer was answered.

We had received during the year $2,986.95 for the support fund; $879.58 for the endowment, and $1,879.75 for the Orphans' Seminary. The support fund had not been hurt (there were thirty-six orphans now) by our building operations.

This fall we lost the services of our faithful and affectionate matron, Miss Annie Starr.

Mrs Lucy Boyd, as full of energy as an egg of meat, took her place among the girls, and unselfish Mrs. Eliza Fuller, among the boys. Our own Laura was enrolled among our teachers. Our Orphanage had at last begun to give to the Church a return for its money.

CHAPTER X.

THE BORDERS ENLARGED.

NO human soul can do a grander thing than to open its doors, welcoming the King of glory in. As each year went by, we saw our children one by one, coming to know Him as their Father. We find that the records of the church contain the names of these fatherless ones on every page. It is a precious privilege to be the means in God's hands of photographing upon the sensitive plate of the orphan's heart, the image of its Redeemer. But there was a joy for which I longed that was possibly even greater than this. How often I had asked of my divine Lord that He would give His Holy Spirit in such measure to His orphans that they should be willing with flaming torches to illumine the way of souls to the cross. When Sam Fulton came to me, and in his plain, straight-forward, matter-of-fact way told me that he asked no higher honor, no greater privilege in this life than to preach the gospel, "Now," said I,

CLINTON COLLEGE.

"Oh Lord, Thou art keeping Thy covenant with Thy servant." I had consecrated this Orphanage to His Church, pleading most earnestly that the gift might be accepted as a means to an end,—and that end, the furtherance of the Lord's work in this world. When I entered the ministry, I believed that I had received the highest office on earth. Eternity will show that to tell men of Jesus Christ is a privilege that angels covet. I now see no higher aim for this Institution than that it should lead its children to seek this post of honor, as commissioned officers to herald salvation to a perishing world.

It was in October, 1880, that the same noble band of Christian workers that had founded the Orphanage, associating others with themselves, had altered the title of their High-School Association by striking out the word High School and inserting College. A charter was obtained, and the Presbyterinn College of South Carolina came into being. In its inception it struggled with many difficulties, against which our beloved and faithful President Lee contended manfully. The wisdom of this organization now became apparent. Mr. Fulton was enrolled among its students and began his preparatory studies. He was to be the first gift of College and Orphanage to the Christian ministry.

In the meanwhile the work on the new Orphans' Seminary went bravely on. Eighty-five thousand feet of lumber, a ton and a half of nails and a thousand wagon loads of stone and sand were used in its construction. Burdette had tied himself to the lofty pinnacle of the steeple, and hanging in mid-air had set in its finial, calling out at the same time, "Yonder the mountains!" Scott had swept his paint brush over all. Riddell looked on his completed job with a satisfied eye. [Ah! he had won the heart of little rosy-cheeked Ella, as the job went on. These carpenters need watching!] Already in our eagerness to observe a holiday, on the 28th of July, (the 28th birth-day of our church), Rev. James H. Thornwell had filled our eyes with tears and brought a glow to our cheeks as his persuasive eloquence filled the Chapel at its dedication. Again orphan voices rang out, and orphan prayers filled the room.

I have before me the "black Ledger" in which were kept the accounts for this building. I read this cheering entry

By cash forward, - - - - - - - - - -	$4,703 75
By Dr. as per acc't. p. - - - - - - -	4,700 00
By cash balance, - - - - - - - - - -	3 75

And then in a brave, bold hand, these lines, unusual in commercial books, are added:

"Oh God, with grateful, humble thanks to Thee for all Thy goodness, I close this account. Thy love has set each stone of this building in its place. Consecrate the house and let its work be glorious, for *Jesus' sake.*"

On the 1st of October, the eleventh year of our work ended and the eighth of our household life. The people gathered that evening in crowds to the Orphans' Chapel. Even the galleries were a dense mass of humanity. The evening train had brought in our honored Governor, Hugh S. Thompson. There was no one in the State that we deemed more suitable than one whose life had been a life spent in educating children and youth, to open formally our school in its new home. He came amid our thanks and went away with our blessings.

The morrow came and the children found themselves in new and better quarters. The old trampling of class on class was done away. Each child knew his place. Three school-rooms instead of one, were filled. In the second story, a handsome collection was formed as the beginning of a Museum; and in the third, the "Nellie Scott" Library already had a thousand volumes, suited for children's reading, on its shelves. Ah! how our children revel in those books.

When the year had ended and we counted up the gifts of God's dear people, we found that they had given us $2,771.25 to provide for our forty-two children: $225.10 for our furnishing fund: and $2,478.71 for the Seminary building. As I read over the list of those who freely gave their treasure for this cause, my heart yearns with love towards them. On page after page, year following year, I find the same familiar names repeated. New ones came in, and they too continue on. Some drop out, and the star against them tells us that their address is changed. They are forever with the Lord. He who cared for them on earth, is caring for them in heaven.

The Seminary was now built and occupied. It had ample room for one hundred and fifty children; that if Museum and Library were elsewhere provided for. Yet our two and forty children filled our two houses even after I had moved my own little family to a cottage that I had built beyond the fence. Whoever would read the signs of God's dealings with us, could see in them this foregone conclusion, that we must lengthen the cords and strengthen the stakes of the tent, that others might come in and get the blessing. And now events suddenly came thick and fast about us.

Before the paint was dry upon the Seminary the busy bees of the Home of Peace were buzzing about our ears, "Our kitchen, our Laundry, our store-room is overcrowded." The very sides of the little rooms they used seemed bursting with the merry laughter of our little cooks and washer-women. We had to build a "Bee-Hive." A thousand flying leaves flew from our press, and the winds boie them North, South, East and West. And then the winds of divide love blew them back, and before October came, half the thousand dollars was laid up in store.

In August of that year, there "happened" (out upon the word!) another thing. Again God touched a Christian woman's heart, and fifteen hundred dollars came with earnest of more to follow, wherewith to build another house, our McCormick Cottage! Never was the finger of God more evident than in this wise foundation. We almost saw Him—we did see Him in His providence.

Events, too, were hastening together in another field, that seemed to call for this new house, that it might do its part in a *new combination.*

But another year was with the recording angel. A new set of workers had taken the place of the old. We had bidden farewell with great regret to Miss Thornwell, (it was the same old, old story of Hymen;) and to our Mrs. Boyd, the very exponent of good sense and energy. Mrs. Simonton's unwearying hand was now at the helm of our domestic affairs; and Mrs. Liddell brought her zeal for knowledge to the help of our orphan-school. There are many good women in God's world and they love to work.

Our Treasurer reported $3,399.26 for the orphans. $1,247.09 for the endowment; $425 for the Bee-Hive;

$286.40 for the Orphans' Seminary building fund; $643.57 for the furnishing fund, and $1500 for the McCormick Cottage. Oh, my soul! praise thou the name of the Lord, thy God. He it is that said, "Open thy mouth wide, and I will fill it."

CHAPTER XI.

OUR TWIN SISTER.

I WAS sitting one evening in company with my two friends, M. S. Bailey and J. W. Copeland. We had covered, in our conversation, the past history of our Orphanage, and the sigh had escaped me, that while we had cultivated God's orphan vineyard, "mine vineyard, which is mine," had I not kept. The school wherein were gathered the children church, was an unsightly barn, and its advantages far inferior to what they should be. Then was discussed also, at length, the value of the united strength that our twins, the Orphanage and the College, might wield for God, if their influence were thrown together. It was shown that we could do nothing without a costly building, costly at least for us. Before we separated, these two gentlemen, with a very little help from the third, had subsctibed $1,350. It was conditioned that the building should be upon the Orphanage premises; that it should be built by Clinton capital; that its administration should be in harmony with that of the Orphanage; that the Orphanage should have the right to four scholarships in its Collegiate department, and that all candidates for the ministry should be educated free of charge. Thus was organized a movement that was to make possible our hope for the education of our orphan boys in the higher branches; to provide an easy highway for those desiring it, into the ministry; and along with it the elevation of the entire community through the establishment of a Christian College in its midst.

But far away to the North matters were also focusing. Mrs. M'Cormick had a friend, a young architect of New York city, Mr. A. Page Brown, who through her, became interested in our work,—a wheel within a wheel. He had already prepared plans for the McCormick Cottage. In the winter of '84 he visited us, and saw our struggles and heard our hopes. Of his own free offer, we soon became possessors of his completed plans for the College building. In the meanwhile the subscription list had swelled to over four thousand dollars.

On the 10th of February, our Bee-Hive with its wind-mill, its furnished Laundry, and its bright new range, completed at a $1,000 cost, with $500 for furnishing, was taken possession of by our girls. One old gentlemen, interested in apiculture, opened wide his mouth before the new building and asked, "What *does* Mr Jacobs want of such a big bee-hive?"

McCORMICK HOME

Another looked with awe-struck surprise at the revolving wheel of the wind-mill, the first that he had ever seen, and asked with a shade of doubt in his voice, "And can that thing raise the wind?" He knows better now.

On the 15th of February, the anniversary of the birth of Hon. C. H. McCormick, Judge J. S. Cothran, now of the U. S. Congress, came to us amid a blinding sleet, and gave an eloquent address on the occasion that should have laid the cornerstone of the McCormick Cottage. The stone was not actually put in place till our now famous festal day, May 28th, when each child put a stone and a trowel full of mortar in the building, and together we sang a hymn of praise to our own God.

It was more than a month before this (11th of April), that the Presbytery of Enoree, in session in the Clinton Church, receded one afternoon from its business. There was a solemn assembly in the Orphans' Chapel. Rev. Robert H. Nall (now of Texas) delivered a glowing appeal on Presbyterian education; Rev. B. G. Clifford, Moderator, then filled the box and gave it to the Chairman of the building Committee. The whole company adjourned to the College site, and the cornerstone of the Clinton Presbyterian College at last was laid. Blessed be God for that day!

And now rang out the sound of hammer and trowel. Our Scott was in his element. Hands were coming and going. Plans were spread out upon the stones, and the building committee puzzled themselves over the great mass of such literature that our New York friend was sending us.

How often in the history of human lives do the bitter providences of God prove to be blessings! We were placing the last trowel full of mortar on the completed College walls. Twenty workmen were in and about them. Then suddenly there was a bowing of the brick pillars in the open arches of the doorways. There was a mighty crash and a great cloud of dust. When this had cleared away, our eyes dazed with the confusion, took in the crushing fact that the whole front of the building lay a mass of stone and broken timber on the ground. Our first thought was for the workmen,—thank God, not a hair of any of them was hurt. And then the second came, how shall we repair this disaster? Our Master answered it by putting into the hearts of the people to treble the amount needed for replacing. Solid stone pillars, filled with historic associations, for they had once upheld the courts of justice at Laurensville, now took the place of the brick. We thanked God for the misfortune and that it came just when it did, instead of a few weeks, months, or years later.

God's work was going on, too, among the orphans. Many this year offered their hearts to Christ. Another of our boys pledged his life, through Presbytery, to the gospel ministry. The list of those who alone were supporting an orphan child was increased to *Nineteen.* The Library had grown to 1600 volumes. We had received when the annual meeting came, $4,419.96 for our orphans; Mrs. McCormick had added $1,050 to her building fund; $1,400 had been received for the Bee-Hive and other purposes; $486.26 had been added to our endowment; a total of more than $7,000. Lord, Thou hast audited the accounts of that year, and Thou knowest how faithfully we sought to make each dime do all that was latent in it.

CHAPTER XII.

"THE REGIONS BEYOND."

IS the reader weary with this story? How much more weary were we with all that stone and lumber! What hours of close and careful planning to make both ends meet! At length, thank God, the work was done. You, reader, reach the consummation easily,—I must cross a year to do it.

Because there was an upheaval of young faces clamoring for their new and cosy class rooms, we opened the College first. They placed the opening on March 15th, my birthday. Thus they told me that I was some day to be only a memory, having laid down forever this busy pen. Why should I not be reminded by such an incident to

> "Louden my cry to God, to men,
> And so fulfil my trust.
> I, too, must lie, breath gone, mouth stopped,
> And silent in the dust!"

But there was only happiness and no fear of the future on that day. President Smith was there, filled with his native earnestness. Prof. Lee saw at last the consummation of his ten years of hope and fear,—the hope realized, the fear gone. Prof. Barnes seemed swimming in a halo of Greek accents and Latin roots. The ladies of the primary department added their charms to the day. We dedicated the house with praise and prayer, and turned it over to the five teachers and a hundred pupils, among whom were four of our orphan household.

I had sometimes thought that my brethren possibly were right when they said that if I ware taken away, this work might stop. The Master proved to me by His tender mercy during this year, that *He* was using me and that He could use another just as well. A friend taking time by the forelock, sent me to get health and wider views in Europe. I was away for months. I returned on that night that the earth throbbed through all our coasts and toppled dear old Charleston from her foundations. It was a joy to find no harm wrought at the Orphanage, and that God's care had been through all those months over our children. For the first August in twelve years the treasury was full and there was no lack of anything. To the endowment, the year had added $749. The support fund had received $4,051.09. The building fund had received $1,254.74.

It was not till the following January (1886), that the great move was made.

All through the fall we had been busy, finishing up Faith Cottage, painting, plastering and whitewashing at the McCormick House, and altering and adorning the Home of Peace. But we had had another project on foot. We had gathered up the remnants of stone and stuff, left over from our greater building and were preparing a tasty house of six rooms for our Printing Office.

Then came the change. Our boys marched out of their old home, and took charge, with a hymn of praise, of their new and handsome hall. They spread out all over it, and because there was room, other orphan lads came and threw in their lot with them. Once more Kit and Bally backed their wagon to the door and carried their heavy loads of type and presses to the fair rooms where they are yet to do noble work.

Then came a troop of little ones,—we call them our "little delights"—and their sweet faces filled Faith Cottage, as their songs, its hall and passages.

They of the Home of Peace, dear girls who bear the heavy burden of the work, settled down to steady duty, and as I walk among them daily, I read in their bright faces lessons about the dear Lord who cares for the sparrows, who says to these orphans, yes, to the humblest among them,—"Ye are of more value than many sparrows."

How quickly fly the years! October, 1887, has passed. It left its precious fruit,—a family of over 50 children, with teachers and officers, 63, It found our farm, with "Uncle Billy" as the children call him, at the head, improved with barns, fences, wood-house, cows with luscious milk, and golden grain, sweeping in soft green waves from hill to hill. A thousand dollars for farm buildings and the like, had been sent in; $4,551.80 for the orphans, and $1,062.45 for the endowment.

I have said but little in these pages about God's work among the heathen. And, yet, next to these dear orphans, and the work in my own church-fold, nothing lies so deeply down among my heart's best loves. It was a joy to see my orphans giving their little mites into the weekly offering. I was glad when our girls came to ask permission that they might organize a Society of their own; for they wanted to share in this great gospel work. But when our dear young brother Fulton, whom God had permitted us to His Church, came with his fixed and settled purpose to bear the cross beyond the Pacific to Japan just waking from the sleep of ages, what could I say? Hesitate? Resist? Only for one moment. Go, dear young brother. God has given us the glorious honor. The honor may like a crown, bear heavily, but it is the King's gift, and we cry Hallelujah!

CHAPTER XIII.

A PREFACE OF THINGS TO COME.

IT is not my time, but your patience, reader, that I would spare. There are a thousand things that I would tell you of our daily life. How often we boys and girls rehearse the incidents of the passing days. We walk among the flowers. We stroll down to the great poplar. We have a hundred little notes to compare about the Anniversary, and the Cornerstone day (May 28th), and Commencement, and Thanksgiving, and Christmas. Oh! Christmas and the Christmas tree and the stockings, the fireworks and the hubbub. It would take a book to tell of that. Sometimes we step into our boys' prayermeeting, or gather for a grand singing in the chapel. Or we bring before us the laughing faces of the Lucy's, the Mary's, the Irene's, the Johnnie's, the Willie's, the Minnie's, the Susie's, the Carrie's, the Hattie's—and—all the rest.

I would like to tell you of our future plans; how we hope some day for other cottages with groups of God's own little ones in them; and for a neat stone

Library building, filled with books and happiness.—How we are planning for a technical school, where the boys will learn to draw and model, and then to execute in wood and iron; and the girls to handle skilfully pencil and graver, and to ring the rapid clicks on telegraph and type-writer; how we are even now building, as each day brings the gifts, our new Memorial Hall, with our true friend, Page Brown, as architect, and *only* our all-glorious Treasurer to provide the funds.

But I write out none of these things. Part of them would unfold the secrets of little hearts; part would trench on prophecy, and part would be just the story of to-day, which is not yet history.

Already, the walls of the new building are nearing completion;—a solid granite structure that will at least out-last every inhabitant now on earth. More than two thousand dollars have been spent upon it; nearly that sum, of which hardly a dollar is on hand, will yet be needed. The work will not stop. *That* is the Lord's method of dealing with us.

As we finish this book, the thirteenth year of our orphan-work is ending. It has been a year of grace. Many of our children have found Jesus to be their own Saviour. God's people have provided for them. For our farm buildings, they gave $588.72, for the Memorial Hall, $2.056.11. To the endowment, the little people of the Sabbath-school added $751.41, while for the care of our *seventy-two* souls, $5,533.64 were poured into our Treasury.

It suits us better, in these closing lines, to turn your thoughts away from the work and the workers to your God and our God,—and to ask you now, as you lay down this book, have we not proved our cause? Is it not true that there is a King in heaven, and that King, our Father who careth for us?

Never was truer word spoken than the assurance the Psalmist took to himself, "I am poor and needy, yet the Lord thinketh upon me." It was a profound faith in this sentiment that inspired the builders of this Orphanage. It is the assurance we have of his presence that maintains the work day by day. We have ceased to recognize any element of doubt in this proposition. It has become to us an axiom. Others may doubt. For us, to doubt would be a crime.

Reader, have you ever doubted Him? If ever you are tempted so again, I beg you step off the train at Clinton. Look southward. You see a tower just to the right of the street, and a square building apparently closing the avenue. Step briskly toward them. Lift the latch and enter the gate. You pass house after house, whose names are now familiar to you, and you hear the ring of hammer and trowel on our new building. And now as you lay your hand on the gray granite or the glittering flint of these houses, say to yourself, It is as true as this solid stone on which my hand resteth, that ALMIGHTY GOD CARETH FOR ME.

www.ingramcontent.com/pod-product-compliance
Lightning Source LLC
Chambersburg PA
CBHW021421090426
42742CB00009B/1208

* 9 7 8 3 7 4 4 7 5 3 1 9 7 *